PRACTICAL HANDBUUK

Of
MEDICINAL CHEMISTRY

BY:

Kunal Bhattacharya, *M. Pharm*
Nongmaithem Randhoni Chanu, *M. Pharm*
Dr.Atanu Bhattacharjee, *M. Pharm, Ph.D*
Dr.Biplab Kumar Dey, *M. Pharm, Ph.D*

**FACULTY OF PHARMACEUTICAL SCIENCES
ASSAM DOWNTOWN UNIVERSITY
2020**

PREFACE

Medicinal chemistry deals with the discovery, design, development and both pharmacological and analytical characterization of drug substances.

The UG students, associated with the myth and reality of '**drug synthesis**' must do an honest attempt to carry out a particular synthesis of a drug substance with a most tried and tested methodical, scientific and rational approach, so that one may get correct and reproducible results for a particular reaction in a flawless manner.

The purpose of this laboratory manual is to introduce undergraduate students to techniques used in medicinal chemistry laboratories and ensure that they master the lab skills necessary to be competitive in the job market.

The handbook presents a collection of twenty one experiments that teach students synthesis of various medicinally important compounds, techniques and purpose of Assays and handling of crucial laboratory equipments and apparatuses. It is hoped, this manual may be a guideline to improve student laboratory skill especially in inorganic laboratory work.

Kunal Bhattacharya
Nongmaithem Randhoni Chanu

Assam, January 2020   *Dr. Atanu Bhattacharjee*
Dr. Biplab Kumar Dey

ACKNOWLEDGEMENT

The editors would like to thank **Assam Downtown University** for providing necessary infrastructure to compile this handbook.

We are grateful to **Amazon Kindle Publisher** for bringing out the volume efficiently to the readers.

The editors are thankful to almighty and families who have encouraged to take up these task and complete it due time. We are also thankful to our friends, academic colleagues for their support in successful accomplishment of the book.

Finally we take the privilege to express our sincere thanks to one and all for their Affection and best wishes for the successful completion of this work.

Our Sincere thanks to all.

Date: 08.01.2020

Kunal Bhattacharya
Nongmaithem Randhoni Chanu
Dr. Atanu Bhattacharjee
Dr. Biplab Kumar Dey

CONTENTS

Introduction to Laboratory Safety

Some rules are NOT made to be broken. That is true of the rules used in a chemistry lab. They are really, truly for your safety and not your humiliation.

Do Not Pipette By Mouth - Ever

You say, "But it's only water." Even if it is, how clean do you think that glassware REALLY is? Using disposable pipettes? I know lots of people who rinse them and put them back! Learn to use the pipette bulb or automated pipetter. Don't pipette by mouth at home either. Gasoline and kerosene should be obvious, but people get hospitalized or die every year, right? I know someone who used his mouth to start the suction on a waterbed to drain it. Do you know what they put in some waterbed additives? Carbon-14. Mmmm...radiation. He couldn't retch fast enough! The lesson is that even seemingly harmless substances may be dangerous!

Read the Chemical Safety Information

A Material Safety Data Sheet (MSDS) should be available for every chemical you use in lab. Read these and follow the recommendations for safe use and disposal of the material.

Dress Appropriately

No sandals, no clothes you love more than life, no contact lenses, and long pants are preferable to shorts or short skirts. Tie long hair back. Wear safety goggles and a lab coat. Even if you aren't clumsy, someone else in the lab probably is. If you take even a few chemistry courses you will probably see people set themselves on fire, spill acid on themselves, others, or notes, splash themselves in the eye, etc. Don't be the bad example to others, remembered for all time for something stupid!

Identify the Safety Equipment

And know how to use it! Given that some people (possibly you) will need them, know the locations of the fire blanket, extinguishers, eyewash, and shower. Ask for demonstrations! If the eyewash hasn't been used in a while the discoloration of the water is usually sufficient to inspire use of safety glasses.

Don't Taste or Sniff Chemicals

For many chemicals, if you can smell them then you are exposing yourself to a dose that can harm you! If the safety information says that a chemical should only be used inside a fume hood, then don't use it anywhere else. This isn't cooking class - don't taste your experiments!

Don't Casually Dispose of Chemicals Down the Drain

Some chemicals can be washed down the drain, while others require a different method of disposal. If a chemical can go in the sink, be sure to wash it away rather than risk an unexpected reaction between chemical 'leftovers' later.

Don't Play Mad Scientist

Don't haphazardly mix chemicals! Pay attention to the order in which chemicals are to be added to each other and do not deviate from the instructions. Even chemicals that mix to produce seemingly safe products should be handled carefully. For example, hydrochloric acid and sodium hydroxide will give you salt water, but the reaction could break your glassware or splash the reactants onto you if you aren't careful!

HAZARD SYMBOLS

Acute Toxic

Health Hazard

Flammable

Exclamation Mark

Flame over circle

Gas Cylinder

Exploding Bomb

Environmental Hazard

Corrosion

LABORATORY GLASSWARES

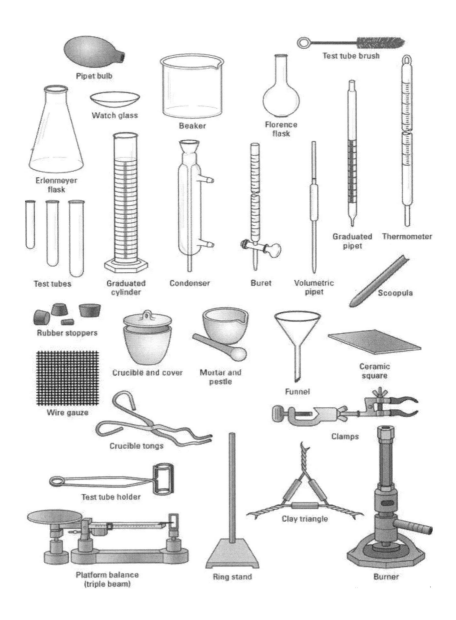

Experiment No:1

SYNTHESIS OF 1,3-PYRAZOLE FROM DIARYLHYDRAZONE AND VICINAL DIOL

Aim: To prepare 1,3-diphenyl pyrazole from diphenyl hydrazone and vicinal diol.

Learning Objectives

To Understand Reactions involved in synthesis of compounds and their medicinal uses

Principle

1,3-substituted pyrazole is prepared by cyclization of diarylhydrazone and vicinal diol in presence of ferric chloride and tert-butylhydroperoxide (TBHP) which is also called regioselective synthesis of substituted pyrazole.

Reaction

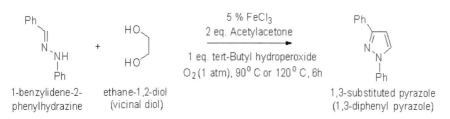

| 1-benzylidene-2-phenylhydrazine | ethane-1,2-diol (vicinal diol) | 5 % $FeCl_3$ 2 eq. Acetylacetone 1 eq. tert-Butyl hydroperoxide O_2 (1 atm), 90° C or 120° C, 6h | 1,3-substituted pyrazole (1,3-diphenyl pyrazole) |

Use: Can be used as antibacterial and antiviral agen

Requirements

A) CHEMICALS

1-benzyledene-2-phenyl hydrazine, Ethane-1,2-diol(ethylene glycol), Ferric chloride, Tert-butyl hydroperoxide, Acetyl acetone, Sodium chloride, Ethyl acetate, Sodium sulphate.

B) APPARATUS

Water-bath, Beaker, Measuring cylinder, Thermometer, Stirrer, Separating funnel, Buchner funnel.

Procedure

About 4.55 g of 1-benzyledene-2-phenyl hydrazine is dissolved in the solution of 25 ml of vicinal diol and ferric chloride (5 mol %). Then another solution of tert-butyl hydroperoxide (5.3 g) in 25 ml of acetyl-acetone is added into it. The mix solution is kept maintaining at a temperature range of 90 to 100° C. The mix solution is left to reach room temperature and stirred for 6 hours. Then the content is poured into water and extracted with ethyl-acetate three times. The combined organic solution is washed with water, then with a saturated solution of sodium chloride, passed through sodium sulphate and evaporated under vacuum.

Report

The percent yield of 1,3-diphenyl pyrazole is......

Experiment No:2

SYNTHESIS OF BENZIMIDAZOLE FROM O-PHENYLENEDIAMINE

Aim: To prepare benzimidazole from o-phenylenediamine

Learning Objectives

To Understand Reactions involved in synthesis of compounds and their medicinal uses

Principle

The two Carbon-nitrogen bonds in benzimidazole when disconnected give o-phenylenediamine and formic acid. Therefore, synthesis of benziemidazole is affected by simply heating the o-phenylenediamine and formic acid together (condensation type of reaction).

Reaction

o-phenylenediamine   Formic acid   Benzimidazole

Use: Antitumor, antifungal, antiparasitic, analgesics, antiviral, antihistamine, as well as used in cardiovascular disease, neurology, endocrinology, and ophthalmology.

Requirements

A) CHEMICALS

o-phenylenediamine , Formic acid (90%), NaOH (10%)

B) APPARATUS

Round bottomed flask (250 ml), Beaker , Measuring cylinder ,Buchner funnel, Filter paper.

Procedure

Place 27 g (0.25 mol) of o-phenylenediamine in a round bottomed flask of 250 ml and add 17.5 g (16 ml, 0.34 mol) of 90% formic acid. Heat the mixture on a water bath at 100 °C for 2 h. Cool and add 10% sodium hydroxide solution slowly, with constant rotation of the flask, until the mixture is just alkaline to litmus. Filter off the synthesized crude benzimidazole by using the pump, wash with ice cold water, drain well and wash again with 25 ml of cold water.

RECRYSTALLISATION

Dissolve the synthesized product in 400 ml of boiling water, add 2 g of decolourising carbon and digest for 15 min. Filter rapidly through a preheated Buchne funnel and a flask at the pump. Cool the filtrate to about 10 °C, filter off the benzimidazole, wash with 25 ml of cold water and dry at 100 °C.

Report

Benzimidazole was synthesized and the percentage yield was found to be......

Experiment No:3

SYNTHESIS OF BENZOTRIAZOLE FROM O-PHENYLENEDIAMINE

Aim: To prepare benzotriazole from o-phenylenediamine

Learning Objectives

To Understand Reactions involved in synthesis of compounds and their medicinal uses

Principle

Benzotriazole can be prepared by treating o-phenylenediamine with nitrous acid (liberated during the reaction between sodium nitrite and acetic acid) to form mono-diazonium salt that follows spontaneous intramolecular cyclization reaction to produce benzotriazole.

Reaction

o- phenylenediamine   Benzotriazole

Use: Used as antifungal, antihypertensive, analgesic

Requirements

A) CHEMICALS

o-phenylenediamine , Glacial acetic acid, Sodium nitrite

B) APPARATUS

Beaker , Measuring cylinder ,Buchner funnel, Filter paper.

Procedure

Dissolve 10.8 g (0.1 mol) of o-phenylenediamine in a mixture of 12 g (11.5 ml, 0.2 mol) of glacial acetic acid and 30 ml of water contained in a 250 ml beaker; slight warming may be necessary. Cool the clear solution to 15 °C, stir magnetically and then add a solution of 7.5 g (0.11mol) of sodium nitrite in 15 ml of water in one portion. The mixture gets warm and reaches a temperature of about 85 °C within 2-3 min and then becomes cool while the colour of the mixture changes from deep red to pale brown. Continue stirring for 15 min, by which time the temperature will have dropped to 35-40 °C, and then thoroughly chill in an ice-water bath for 30 min. Collect the product by vacuum filtration of the pale brown solid which separates and wash with three 30 ml portions of ice cold water.

RECRYSTALLISATION

Dissolve the solid in about 130 ml of boiling water, add decolourising charcoal, filter and allow the filtrate to cool to about 50 °C before adding a few crystals of the synthesized product (benzotriazole) which have been retained for seeding. Allow the mixture to attain room temperature slowly to avoid separation of the material as an oil) and then thoroughly chill in ice and collect the benzotriazole which separates as pale straw-coloured needles, m.p. 99-100 °C. A second crop may be obtained by concentrating the filtrate. The yield is about 8 g (67%). The benzotriazole crystallises much more readily from benzene (55 ml) but the material is still slightly coloured. A pure white product can be obtained by sublimation at 90-95 °C at 0.2 mmHg.

Report

Benzotriazole was synthesized and the percentage yield was found to be......

Experiment No:4

SYNTHESIS OF 2,3- DIPHENYLQUINOXALINE

Aim: To prepare 2,3- diphenylquinoxaline from benzyl.

Learning Objectives

To Understand Reactions involved in synthesis of compounds and their medicinal uses

Principle

This is a method of condensation of an aryl 1,2-diamine with a 1,2-dicarbonyl compound by heating in a solvent like rectified sprit. Here condensation reaction of 1,2-diamines with α-diketones occurs with cyclization.

Reaction

o-phenylenediamine   Benzil   2,3- diphenylquinoxaline

Use: Used as anti-viral, anti-bacterial, anti-inflammatory, anti-protozoal, anti-cancer (colon cancer therapies), antidepressant, anti-HIV agent and as kinase inhibitor

Requirements

A) CHEMICALS

o-phenylenediamine, Benzil, Rectified sprit

B) APPARATUS

Beaker, Measuring cylinder ,Buchner funnel, Filter paper.

Procedure

To a warm solution of 2.1 g (0.01 mol) of benzil in 8 ml of rectified spirit, mix a solution of 1.1 g (0.01 mol) of o-phenylenediamine in 8 ml rectified spirit. Warm in a water bath for 30 min, add water until a slight cloudiness persists and allow to cool. Filter and recrystallise from aqueous ethanol.

Report

2,3-diphenylquinoxaline was synthesized and the percentage yield was found to be……

Experiment No:5

SYNTHESIS OF ETHYL P-AMINOBENZOATE (BENZOCAINE) FROM P- NITROBENZOIC ACID

Aim: To prepare Benzocaine from p- nitrobenzoic acid.

Learning Objectives

To Understand Reactions involved in synthesis of compounds and their medicinal uses

Principle

This experiment has two steps.

Step 1: preparation of p-aminobenzoic acid from p-nitrobenzoic acid

Step 2: preparation of ethyl p-aminobenzoate from p-aminobenzoic acid

In step 1 common reduction of aromatic para-nitrobenzoic acid by tin and hydrochloric acid to para-aminobenzoic acid and in step 2 esterification of para-aminobenzoic acid by sulphuric acid and ethanol to benzocaine occurring called Fischer esterification.

Reactions

Step 1:

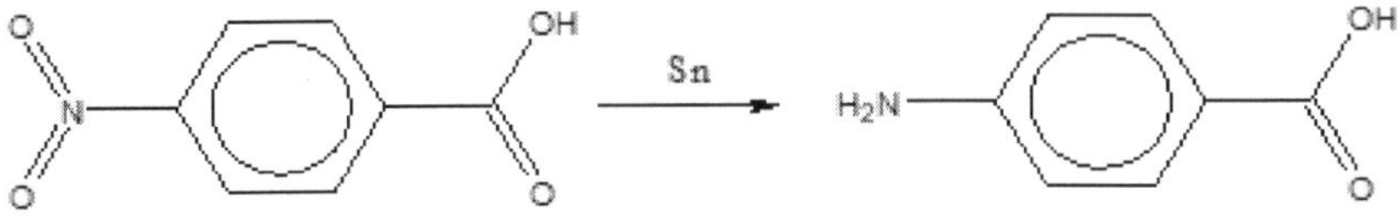

Step 2:

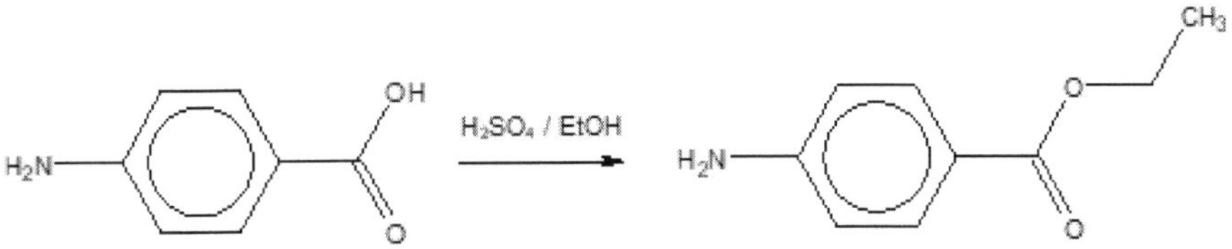

Use: Used as a local anesthetic agent.

Requirements

A) CHEMICALS

p-Nitrobenzoic acid, Tin powder, Conc. HCl, Conc. Ammonia, Celite (filter aid), Glacial acetic acid, Prepared p-aminobenzoic acid, Absolute ethanol, Sodium carbonate.

B) APPARATUS

Round bottomed flask – 1 litre, Reflux condenser set, Gas inlet tube, Beaker, Buchner funnel, Measuring cylinder, Filter paper, Litmus paper

Procedure Step 1: Preparation of p-aminobenzoic acid

Place 15 g (0.09 mol) of p-nitrobenzoic acid in a 1-litre round-bottomed flask fitted with a reflux condenser. Introduce 35 g (0.295 mol) ofvpowdered tin and 75 ml of concentrated hydrochloric acid. Heat the mixture gently until the reaction commences, and remove the flame. Shake the flask frequently and take care that the insoluble acid adhering to the sides of the flask is transferred to the reaction mixture: occasional gentle warming may be necessary. After about 20 min, most of the tin will have reacted and a clear solution remains. Allow to cool somewhat and decant the liquid into a 1-litre beaker; wash the residual tin by decantation with 15 ml of water, and add the washings to the contents of the beaker. Add concentrated ammonia solution (d 0.88) until the solution is just alkaline to litmus and digest the suspension of precipitated hydrated tin oxide on a steam bath for 20 min. Add 10 g of filter-aid ('Celite'), stir well, filter at the pump and wash with hot water. Transfer the filter cake to a beaker, heat on a water bath with 200 ml of water to ensure extraction of the product and refilter. Concentrate the combined filtrate and washings until the volume has been reduced to 175-200 ml: filter off any solid which separates.Acidify the liquid to litmus with glacial acetic acid and evaporate on a water bath until crystals commence to separate; cool in ice, filter the crystals at the pump and dry in the steam oven.

Step 2: **Preparation of ethyl p-aminobenzoate (esterification of p-aminobenzoic acid)**

Place 80 ml of absolute ethanol in a 250 ml two-necked flask equipped with a double surface reflux condenser and a gas inlet tube. Pass dry hydrogen chloride through the alcohol until saturated; the increase in weight is about 20 g; remove the gas inlet tube, introduce 12 g (0.088 mol) of p-aminobenzoic acid and heat the mixture under reflux for 2 hours. Upon cooling, the reaction mixture sets to a solid mass of the hydrochloride of ethyl p-aminobenzoate. It is better, however, to pour the hot solution into 300 ml of water (no hydrochloride separates) and add solid sodium carbonate carefully to the clear solution until it is neutral to litmus. Filter off the precipitated ester at the pump and dry in the air.

Report

Benzocaine was synthesized and the percentage yield was found to be......

Experiment No:6

Synthesis of phenytoin from benzil and urea

Aim: To prepare phenytoin from benzil and urea.

Learning Objectives

To Understand Reactions involved in synthesis of compounds and their medicinal uses

Principle

Base catalyzed reaction between benzyl and urea is used for synthesis of phenytoin. The reaction is proceeding via intramolecular cyclization to form an intermediate heterocylic pinacol, which on acidification yield hydantoin (phenytoin) as a result of 1,2-diphenyl shift in pinacol rearrangement reaction.

Reactions

Use: It is a common antiepileptic drug

Requirements

A) CHEMICALS

Benzil,   Urea,   Sodium   hydroxide,   Ethanol, Concentrated hydrochloric acid

B) APPARATUS

Round-bottom flask – 100 ml, Reflux condenser, Crystallizing dish – 500 ml, Heating mantle, Stirrer, Beaker – 400 ml, Filtering flask with Büchner funnel, Graduated cylinders – 100 ml and 50 ml, Petri dish

Procedure

Place 5.3 g (0.025 mol) of benzil, 3.0 g (0.05 mol) of urea, 15 ml of aqueous sodium hydroxide solution (30%) and 75 ml of ethanol in a round bottomed flask of 100 ml capacity. Set up a reflux condenser with the flask and boil using an electric heating mantle for at least 2 h. Cool to room temperature, pour the reaction mixture into 125 ml of water and mix carefully. Allow the reaction mixture to stand for 15 min and then filter the product under suction to remove an insoluble by-product. Render the filtrate strongly acidic with concentrated hydrochloric acid, cool in ice-water and immediately filter off the precipitated product under suction. Recrystallise at least once from industrial spirit.

Report

Phenytoin was synthesized and the percentage yield was found to be.......

Experiment No:7

PREPARATION OF PHENOTHIAZINE

Aim: To prepare phenothiazine from diphenylamine.

Learning Objectives

To Understand Reactions involved in synthesis of compounds and their medicinal uses

Principle

Phenothiazine is prepared by fusing diphenylamine with sulphur with rapid evolution of hydrogen sulphide.

Reactions

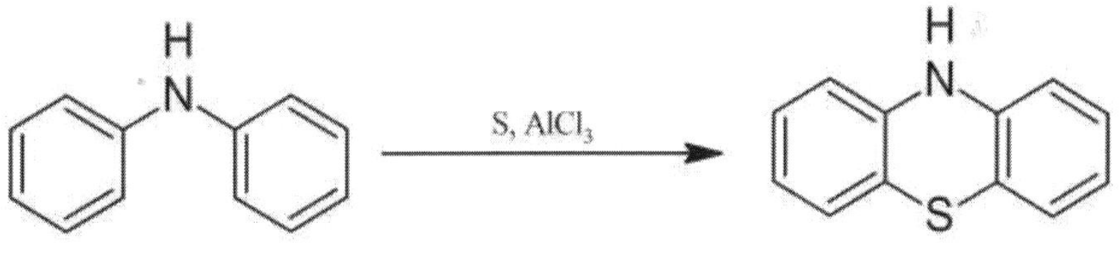

Use: It is used as a antipsychotic.

Requirements

A) CHEMICALS

Diphenylamine, Sulphur, anhydrous calcium chloride, alcohol.

B) APPARATUS

Beaker, Buchner funnel, measuring cylinder, filter paper.

Procedure

22 g of diphenylamine, 8.2 g of sulphur and 3.2 g of anhydrous calcium chloride are melted together. The reaction sets 140-150 °C with the rapid evolution of hydrogen sulphide; by lowering the temperature, a few degrees the reaction can be slackened. When the reaction has moderated, the temperature is raised to 160 °C for a time. The melt, when cool, is ground up and extracted, first with water and then with dilute alcohol. The residue consists of almost pure phenothiazine. It can be recrystallised from alcohol.

Report

Phenothiazine was synthesized and the percentage yield was found to be......

Experiment No:8

PREPARATION OF BARBITURIC ACID

Aim: To prepare Barbituric Acid

Learning Objectives

To Understand Reactions involved in synthesis of compounds and their medicinal uses

Principle

The synthesis of barbituric acid is affected by condensation of diethyl malonate with urea in the presence of sodium ethoxide which may be prepared by reacting Na metal with ethanol and it undergo cyclization reaction with diethyl malonate.

Reactions

| Diethyl malonate | Urea | Barbituric acid |

Use: It is used as a hypnotics, sedatives, anticonvulsants.

Requirements

A) CHEMICALS

Sodium metal, Ethanol, Diethyl malonate, Urea, Calcium chloride, Concentrated hydrochloric acid.

B) APPARATUS

Round bottom flask – 2000 ml, Reflux condenser, Beaker,

Buchner funnel, Measuring cylinder, filter paper

Procedure

Assemble a double surface reflux condenser with a 2 litre round bottomed flask, place 11.5g of clean sodium. Mix 250 ml of absolute ethanol in a portion and if the reaction is unduly vigorous, immerse the flask within ice. When all the sodium has completed reaction, add diethyl malonate 80 g (76 ml), followed by a solution of dry urea 30 g in 250 ml of hot (70 °C) absolute ethanol. Shake the mixture thoroughly, attach a calcium chloride guard tube to the top of the condenser, start reflux of the mixture for 7 h in an oil bath and heat to 110 °C. A white solid will be separated. Treat the reaction mixture with hot (50 °C) water 450 ml and then with concentrated hydrochloric acid, with constant stirring, until the solution will be acid (about 45 ml).

Filter the resulting almost clear solution and leave it in the refrigerator overnight. Filter the solid at the pump, wash it with 25 ml of cold water, drain well and then dry at 100 °C for 4 hours.

Report

Barbituric acid was synthesized and the percentage yield was found to be…..

Experiment No:9

SYNTHESIS OF SULPHANILAMIDE

Aim: To synthesize and submit sulphanilamide from Acetanilide.

Learning Objectives

To Understand Reactions involved in synthesis of compounds and their medicinal uses

Principle

Acetanilide undergoes chlorosulfonation by reacting with chlorosulfonic acid and there by obtained sulphonyl chloride reacts with ammonia solution to yield sulphonamide where the acetoxy group attached to the para position of sulphonamide gets detaches as acetylchloride by reacting with hydrochloric acid to offer Sulphanilamide.

Reaction

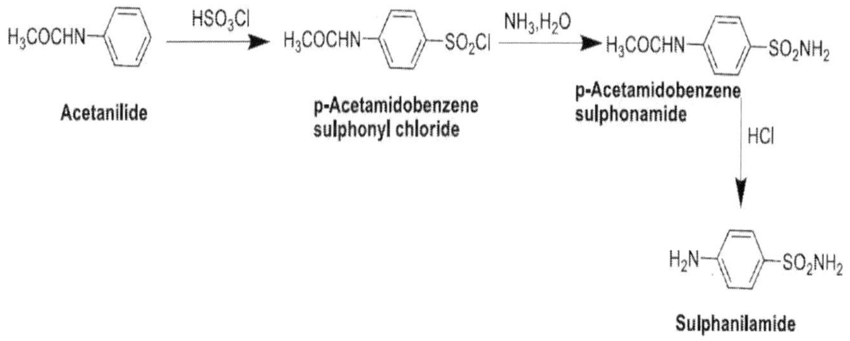

| Acetanilide | p-Acetamidobenzene sulphonyl chloride | p-Acetamidobenzene sulphonamide |

Sulphanilamide

Use: Antibiotic.

Requirements

A) CHEMICALS

Acetanilide, Chlorosulphonic acid, Ammonia, Ethanol, Hydrochloric Acid.

B) APPARATUS

500-ml two-necked flask, dropping funnel, reflux condenser, Water-bath, Beaker, Measuring cylinder, Stirrer, funnel.

Procedure for preparation of p-Acetamidobenzenesulphonyl chloride

500-ml two-necked flask with a dropping funnel and a reflux condenser attach the top of the latter to a device for the absorption of hydrogen chloride. Place 20g of dry acetanilide in the flask and 50ml of a good grade of chlorosulphonic acid in the dropping funnel and insert a calcium chloride guard-tube into the latter. Add the chlorosulphonic acid in small portions and shake the flask from time to time to ensure thorough mixing. When the addition has been made, heat the reaction mixture on a water bath for1 hour in order to complete the reaction. Allow to cool and pour the oily mixture in a thin stream with stirring into 30g of crushed ice (or icewater) contained in a 1-litre beaker. Carryout this operation carefully in the fume cupboard since the excess of Chlorosulphonic acid reacts vigorously with the water.

Rinse the flask with a Little ice-water and add the rinsings to the contents of the beaker. Breakup any lumps of solid material and stir the mixture for several minutes in order to obtain an even suspension of the granular white solid. Filter off the p–acetamido benzene

sulphonyl chloride at the pump and wash it with a little cold water; press and drain well. Use the crude product immediately in the next stage.

p-Acetamidobenzenesulphonamide:-

Transfer the crude p-acetamidobenzenesulphonylchloride to the rinsed reaction flask, and add a mixture of 70ml of concentrated ammonia solution and 70ml of water. Mix the contents of the flask thoroughly, and heat the mixture with occasional swirling (fume cupboard) to just below the boiling point for about 15 minutes. The sulphonyl chloride will be converted into a pasty suspension of the corresponding sulphonamide. Cool the suspension in ice, and then add dilute sulphuric acid until the mixture is just acid to Congo red paper. Collect the

product on a Buchner funnel, wash with a little cold water and drain as completely as possible. It is desirable, but not essential, to dry the crude p-acetamido benzene sulphonamide at100°C.

p-Aminobenzenesulphonamide:-

Transfer the crude p-acetamidobenzenesulphonamide to a 500-ml flask, add 10ml of concentrated hydrochloric acid and 30ml of water. Boil the mixture gently under reflux for 30-45 minutes. The solution, when cooled to room temperature, should deposit no solid amide; if a solid separates, heat for a further short period. Treat the cooled solution with 2g of decolourising carbon, heat the mixture to boiling and filter with suction through a hardened filter paper.

Place the filtrate (a solution of sulphanilamide hydrochloride) in a litre beaker and cautiously add 16g of solid sodium hydrogen carbonate in portions with stirring.After the evolution of gas has subsided, test the suspension with litmus paper and if it is still acid, add more sodium hydrogen carbonate until neutral. Cool in ice, filter off the sulphanilamide with suction and dry.

Report

Sulphanilamide was prepared and submitted in the laboratory and its yield was found to be......

Experiment No:10

SYNTHESIS OF 7-HYDROXY-4-METHYL COUMARIN

Aim: To synthesize 7-hydroxy-4-methyl coumarin.

Learning Objectives

To Understand Reactions involved in synthesis of compounds and their medicinal uses

Principle

A general synthesis of coumarins involves the interaction of a phenol with a β-ketoester in presence of an acid condensing agent (Pechmann reaction). Concentrated sulphuric acid is usually used as the condensing agent for simple monohydric phenols and β-ketoesters, although phenol itself reacts better in the presence of aluminium chloride. The mechanism of the reaction is thought to involve the initial formation of a β-hydroxy ester, which then cyclises and dehydrates to yield the coumarin. Polyhydric phenols, particularly here the two hydroxyl groups are meta oriented, react with great ease and sulphuric acid is used as the condensing agent with careful temperature control to ensure a good yield.

Reaction

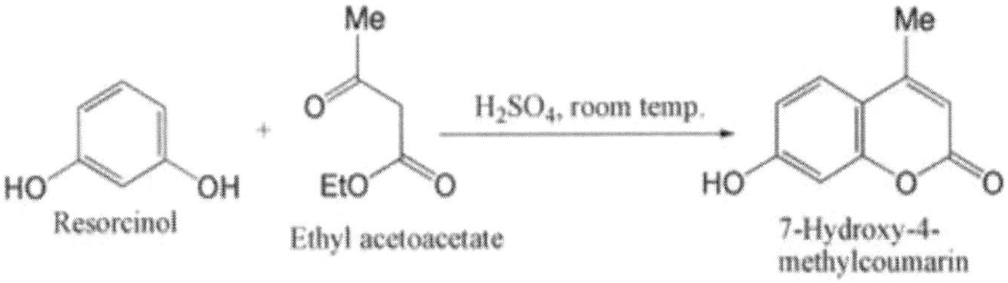

Use: It is used commercially as laser dye. It is also the starting material for the production of the insecticide 'hymecromone'.

Requirements

A) CHEMICALS

Conc. sulphuric acid, Resorcinol, Ethyl acetoacetate, Ice, Sodium hydroxide solution (5%), Sulphuric acid (2 M), Ethanol 95%

B) APPARATUS

Three necked flask – 3 litres, Thermometer, Mechanical stirrer, A dropping funnel, Beaker, Buchner funnel, Measuring cylinder, Filter paper

Procedure

Take 1 litre of concentrated sulphuric acid in a 3 litres capacity 3 necked flask fitted with a thermometer, mechanical stirrer and a dropping funnel. Immerse the flask in an ice bath. When the temperature falls below 10 °C, add a solution of 100 g (0.91 mol) of resorcinol in 134g (130.5 ml, 1.03 mol) of redistilled ethyl acetoacetate drop wise and with stirring. Maintain the temperature below 10 °C by means of an ice-salt bath during the addition (2 h).

Keep the mixture at room temperature for 18 h and then pour it into a mixture of 2 kg of crushed ice with vigorous stirring and 3 litres of water. Collect the precipitate by suction filtration and wash it with three 25 ml portions of cold water. Dissolve the solid in 1500 ml of 5 percent sodium hydroxide solution, filter and add dilute 2 M sulphuric acid (about 550 ml) with vigorous stirring until the solution is acid to litmus. Filter the crude 4-methyl-7-hydroxycoumarin at the pump, wash with four 25 ml portions of cold water and dry at 100 °C. Recrystallise from 95 percent ethanol. The pure compound separates in colourless needles.

Report

7-hydroxy-4-methyl coumarin was prepared and submitted in the laboratory and its yield was found to be......

Experiment No:11

SYNTHESIS OF CHLOROBUTANOL

Aim: To synthesize Chlorobutanol.

Learning Objectives

To Understand Reactions involved in synthesis of compounds and their medicinal uses

Principle

Chlorobutanol (trichloro-2-methyl-2-propanol) is obtained by the nucleophilic attack of carbanion formed from choroform in the alkaline medium on the partially positively charged carbon of acetone.It used at a concentration of 0.5% where it lends long term stability to multi-ingredient formulations. However, it retains antimicrobial activity at 0.05% in water. It is a white, volatile solid with a menthol-like odor. Chlorobutanol is extremely volatile even at ordinary temperatures, and requires to be dried with great care to avoid loss.

Reaction

$$\underset{\underset{\displaystyle CH_3}{H_3C}}{\overset{\displaystyle O}{\|}} + CHCl_3 \xrightarrow{\text{KOH}} \underset{\underset{\displaystyle CH_3}{H_3C}}{\overset{\displaystyle Cl_3C \quad OH}{\times}}$$

Use: Sedative, Hypnotic, antibacterial and antifungal

Requirements

A) CHEMICALS

Acetone, Chloroform, Potassium hydroxide, ice cold water, ethanol

B) APPARATUS

Stirrer, Beaker, Measuring cylinder, Filter paper

Procedure

Combine 90 mL of acetone, 10 mL of chloroform and 2 g of potassium hydroxide, stir the mixture vigorously at -5°C for 2h. After which the suspension was filtered, the filter needs to be washed with acetone, then distill at 60°C until the weight of the solution remains constant. Then pour the chlorobutanol into a bigger beaker and add 100 mL of ice-cold water. Filter and store the filtered sludge. Recrystallize in ethanol to get pure solid chlorobutanol hemihydrate crystals.

Report

Chlorobutanol was prepared and submitted in the laboratory and its yield was found to be......

Experiment No:12

SYNTHESIS OF HEXAMINE

Aim: To synthesize Hexamine

Learning Objectives

To Understand Reactions involved in synthesis of compounds and their medicinal uses

Principle

Hexamethylenetetramine or methenamine, also known as hexamine or urotropin, is a heterocyclic organic compound with the formula $(CH_2)_6N_4$. This white crystalline compound is highly soluble in water and polar organic solvents. It has a cage-like structure.It is prepared industrially by combining formaldehyde and ammonia.The reaction can be conducted in gas phase and in solution. The molecule behaves like an amine base, undergoing protonation and N-alkylation

Reaction

$$6CH_2O + 6NH_3 \longrightarrow \text{(hexamine cage structure)} + 6H_2O$$

Use: used for the treatment of urinary tract infection

Requirements

A) CHEMICALS

Conc. Formaldehyde, 30% ammonium hydroxide solution, ice cold water, ethanol

B) APPARATUS

Stirrer, Beaker, Measuring cylinder, Filter paper, water bath

Procedure

To a beaker immersed in an ice bath add 200 mL of conc. formaldehyde and start adding slowly 320 mL of 30 % ammonium hydroxide solution, the temperature must be kept below 20°C. Then evaporate the water off by heating the flask in a hot water bath, recrystallize the hexamine in hot ethanol.

Report

Hexamine was prepared and submitted in the laboratory and its yield was found to be......

Experiment No:13

SYNTHESIS OF TRIPHENYL- IMIDAZOLE

Aim: To synthesize 2,4,5-triphenyl-1*H*-imidazole

Learning Objectives

To Understand Reactions involved in synthesis of compounds and their medicinal uses

Principle

A simple highly versatile and efficient synthesis of 2,4,5-trisubstituted imidazoles is achieved by three component cyclocondensation of 1,2-dicarbonyl compounds, aldehydes and ammonium acetate as ammonia source in thermal solvent free condition using Brønsted acidic ionic liquid diethyl ammonium hydrogen phosphate as catalyst. The key advantages of this process are cost effectiveness of catalyst, reusability of catalyst, easy work-up and purification of products by non-chromatographic methods, excellent yields and very short time reactions.

Reaction

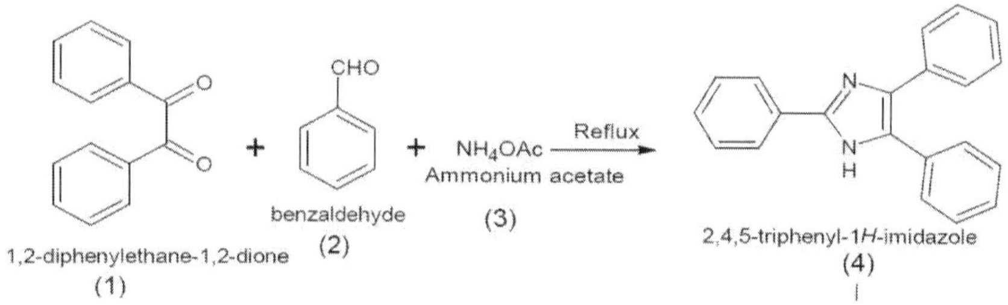

1,2-diphenylethane-1,2-dione (1) + benzaldehyde (2) + NH₄OAc (Ammonium acetate) (3) → (Reflux) 2,4,5-triphenyl-1H-imidazole (4)

Use: used for the treatment of urinary tract infection

Requirements

A) CHEMICALS

Benzil, Benzaldehyde, Ammonium acetate, Ethanoic acid, Ammonium Hydroxide, Aqueous ethanol.

B) APPARATUS

250ml round bottom flask ,Magnetic Stirrer, Beaker, Measuring cylinder, Filter paper, oil bath

Procedure

Benzil (25mmol), Benzaldehyde (25mmol) and ammonium acetate (130mmol) was dissolved in 100ml ethanoic acid (100%) in 250ml round bottom flask containing a magnetic stirrer bar and was heated at the mixture to reflux in oil bath for 1hr with stirring. After this time the mixture was cooled to room temperature and was filtered to remove precipitate which may be present. 500ml of water was added to filtrate and collected the precipitate by filtration with suction.

Filtrate was neutralized with Ammonium Hydroxide and second crop of solid was collected. The two crop of solid was combined and recrystallized from aqueous ethanol.

Report

Triphenyl-imidazole was prepared and submitted in the laboratory and its yield was found to be......

Experiment No:14

ASSAY OF CHLORPROMAZINE HCL

Aim: To determine percentage purity of chlorpromazine HCl.

Learning Objectives

To understand the basic principle behind assay of compounds along with medicinal uses of compounds.

Principle

The assay of chlorpromazine HCl can be carried out by using non-aqueous titration. In

the assay of chlorpromazine methyl orange used as indicator.

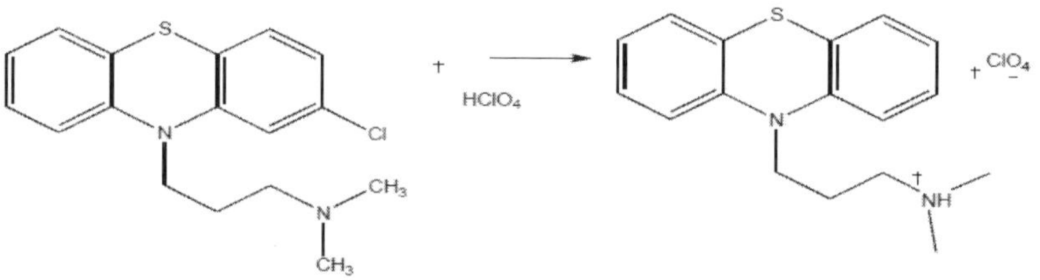

Use: Used to treat psychotic disorders

Requirements

A) CHEMICALS

Acetone, 0.1 M Perchloric acid, Methyl orange etc.

B) APPARATUS

Beaker, Pipette, Burette, measuring cylinder, conical flask etc.

Procedure

Weigh accurately about 0.6 g, dissolve in 200 ml of acetone and add 15 ml of mercuric

acetate solution. Titrate with 0.1 M perchloric acid, using a saturated solution of methyl

orange in acetone as indicator. Carry out a blank titration.

1 ml of 0.1 M perchloric acid is equivalent to 0.03553 g of chlorpromazine hydrochloride.

$$\text{Percentage purity} = \frac{(\text{Titre value x molarity of perchloric acid x Eq.factor}) \times 100}{\text{Weight taken x expected molarity}}$$

Report

The % purity of chlorpromazine HCl was found to be......

Experiment No:15

ASSAY OF ATROPINE SULPHATE

Aim: To determine percentage purity of Atropine

Learning Objectives

To understand the basic principle behind assay of compounds along with medicinal uses of compounds.

Principle

The assay of atropine sulphate was carried out by using endpoint potentiometry. 0.1 M perchloric acid is used for titration.

Use: Used to treat psychotic disorders

Requirements

A) CHEMICALS

Acetone, 0.1 M Perchloric acid, Methyl orange etc..

B) APPARATUS

Beaker, Pipette, Burette, measuring cylinder, conical flask etc.

Procedure

Weigh 0.5 g, dissolve in 30 ml of anhydrous glacial acetic acid. Titrate with 0.1 M perchloric acid, determining the end-point potentiometrically. Carry out a blank titration.1 ml of 0.1 M perchloric acid is equivalent to 0.06768 g of atropine sulphate.

Percentage purity= $\dfrac{\text{(Titre value x molarity of perchloric acid x Eq.factor) x 100}}{\text{Weight taken x expected molarity}}$

Report

The % purity of Atropine Sulphate was found to be......

Experiment No:16

ASSAY OF IBUPROFEN

Aim: To determine percentage purity of Atropine

Learning Objectives

To understand the basic principle behind assay of compounds along with medicinal uses of compounds.

Principle

The principle involoved in the assay of Ibuprofen is acid-base titration where the acidic group in Ibuprofen is neutralized by titrating with base i.e. NaOH using phenolphthalein as an indicator where the end point is colourless to pink.

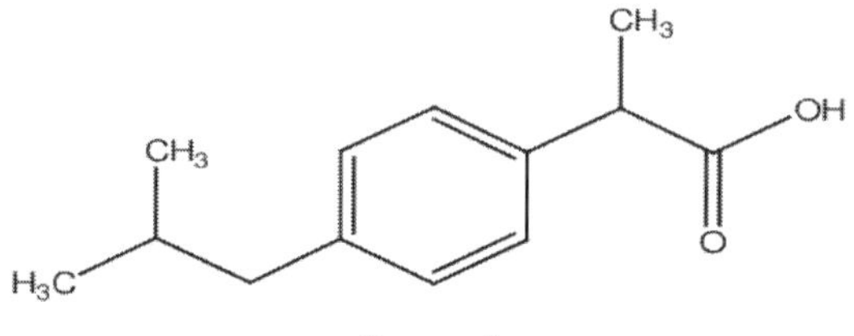

Ibuprofen

Use: Antiinflammatory

Requirements

A) CHEMICALS

Ibuprofen, sodium hydroxide, Potassium hydrogen pthallate, Phenolpthalein indicator,

Phenol red etc.,

B) APPARATUS

Erlenmeyer flask, Volumetric flask, Pipette, Burette etc.,

Procedure

Standardization of 0.1 M NaOH:

Weigh about 0.5gm of KHP into 250-mL Erlenmeyer flask which was previously powdered and dried at 1100C. Dissolve the sample in about 30 mL of distilled water before you titrate. Add five drops of phenolphthalein indicator and titrate with 0.1M NaOH by constant swirling to the first appearance of a permanent pink color.

Each mL of 0.1M NaOH is equivalent to 0.02042gm of $C_8H_5KO_4$.

Assay: Weigh accurately about 0.5gm of drug and dissolve in 100ml of ethanol (95%) and titrate with a 0.1m NaOH using phenolphthalein as an indicator where the end point is permanent pink colour. Repeat the titration with blank.

Each mL of 0.1M NaOH is equivalent to 0.02663gm of $C_{13}H_{18}O_2$.

Percentage purity= $\dfrac{\text{(Titre value x molarity of NaOH x Eq.factor) x 100}}{\text{Weight taken x expected molarity}}$

Report

The percentage purity of Ibuprofen was found to be……

Experiment No:17

ASSAY OF DAPSONE

Aim: To determine percentage purity of Dapsone

Learning Objectives

To understand the basic principle behind assay of compounds along with medicinal uses of compounds.

Principle

The first involved is addition of sodium nitrite to hydrochloric acid cause formation of nitrous acid.

$$NaNO_2 + HCl \longrightarrow HONO + NaCl$$

This nitrous acid diazotises the aromatic amino group

$$R - NH2 + NaNO_2 + HCl \longrightarrow R - N+ \equiv N^- Cl^- + NaCl^+$$

Use: Used to treat a certain type of skin disorder (dermatitis herpetiformis)

Requirements

A) CHEMICALS

Water, Hydrochloric acid, Sodium Nitrite Solution

B) APPARATUS

Beaker, Pipette, Burette, measuring cylinder, conical flask etc.

Procedure

Weigh accurately about 0.3 g and dissolve in a mixture of 20 ml of water and 20 ml of hydrochloric acid. Cool the solution to about 15° and determine by the nitrite titration. Carry out a blank titration. 1 ml of 0.1 M sodium nitrite is equivalent to 0.01242 g of $C_{12}H_{12}N_2O_2S$.

$$\text{Percentage purity} = \frac{(\text{Titre value} \times \text{molarity of sodium nitrite} \times \text{Eq.factor}) \times 100}{\text{Weight taken} \times \text{expected molarity}}$$

Report

The % purity of Dapsone was found to be......

Experiment No:18

ASSAY OF METRONIDAZOLE

Aim: To determine percentage purity of Metronidazole

Learning Objectives

To understand the basic principle behind assay of compounds along with medicinal uses of compounds.

Principle

Water behaves as both a weak acid and a weak base thus, in an aqueous

environment, it can compete effectively with very weak acids and bases with regard to proton donation and acceptance, as shown below:

$H_2O + H^+ \rightleftharpoons H_3O^+$

Competes with $RNH_2 + H \rightarrow RNH_3^+$

or

$H_2O + B \rightleftharpoons OH^- + BH^+$

Competes with ROH + B RO⁻ + BH+ which makes the endpoint detection relatively more difficult. That's why very weak acid/base can't be titrated in water. So, A general rule is estimated that bases with pKa < 7 or acids with pKa > 7 cannot be determined accurately in aqueous solution.

Brønsted-Lowry theory is used in non-aqueous titration. According to this theory an acid is a proton donor, i.e. a substance which tends to dissociate to yield a proton, and a base is proton acceptor, i.e. a substance which tends to combine with a proton. When an acid HB dissociates it yields a proton together with the conjugate base B of the acid:

$$HB \rightleftharpoons H^+ + B^-$$

acid proton base

Alternatively, the base B will combine with a proton to yield the conjugate acid HB of the base B, for every base has its conjugate acid and, every acid has its conjugate base.

+ HClO₄ ⟶

Use: Antibiotic

Requirements

A) CHEMICALS

Perchloric acid, Glacial acetic acid, Acetic anhydride, Potassium hydrogen phthalate, crystal violet

Beaker, Pipette, Burette, measuring cylinder, conical flask etc.

Procedure

Preparation of 0.1 N Perchloric acid ($HClO_4$):

Gradually mixed 8.5 ml of perchloric acid to 900 ml of glacial acetic acid with

vigorous and continuous stirring. After that added 30 ml acetic anhydride and make up the volume to 1 litre with glacial acetic acid and allow to stand for 24 hours before use.

Standardization of 0.1 N Perchloric Acid :

Weighed accurately about 0.5 g of potassium hydrogen phthalate in a 100 ml conical flask. And added 25 ml of glacial acetic acid and attached a reflux condenser fitted with a silica-gel drying tube. Warmed until the salt gets dissolved completely. Cooled and titrated with 0.1 N perchloric acid where crystal violet (2 drops) is used as an indicator. (end point Blue to Blue-Green (0.5% w/v)).

Assay of metronidazole :

Weighed accurately about 0.3 g of metronidazole sample into a 250 ml conical flask; added Glacial acetic acid (50 ml), warmed gently. Cooled and titrated with 0.1 N perchloric acid using α - Naphtol benzein as indicator.

17.12 mg or 0.01712 g of C6H9N3O3 ≡ 1 ml of 0.1 N HClO₄

Percentage purity= $\dfrac{(\text{Titre value} \times \text{Normality} \times \text{Eq.factor}) \times 100}{\text{Weight taken} \times \text{expected Normality}}$

Report

The % purity of Metronidazole was found to be…..

Experiment No:19

ASSAY OF CHLOROQUINE

Aim: To determine percentage purity Chloroquine phosphate

Learning Objectives
To understand the basic principle behind assay of compounds along with medicinal uses of compounds.

Principle
Potentiometric titration is a technique similar to direct titration of a redox reaction. It is a useful means of characterizing an acid. No indicator is used; instead the potential is measured across the analyte, typically an electrolyte solution. Chloroquine is a medication used to prevent and to treat malaria in areas where malaria is known to be sensitive to its effects.

Use: Antimalarial

Requirements

A) CHEMICALS

Perchloric acid, Anhydrous glacial acetic acid

B) APPARATUS

Beaker, Pipette, Burette, measuring cylinder, conical flask etc.

Procedure

Weigh accurately about 0.2 g and dissolve in 50 ml of anhydrous glacial acetic acid with the aid of heat (if necessary, heat under a reflux condenser). Titrate with 0.1 M perchloric acid, determining the end-point potentiometrically . Carry out a blank titration.

1 ml of 0.1 M perchloric acid is equivalent to 0.02579 g of $C_{18}H_{26}CIN_3,2H_3PO_4$.

Percentage purity= (Titre value x molarity of perchloric acid x Eq.factor) x 100

$$\frac{}{\text{Weight taken x expected molarity}}$$

Report

The % purity of Chloroquine phosphate was found to be......

Experiment No:20

ASSAY OF CHLORPHENIRAMINE MALEATE

Aim: To determine percentage purity Chlorpheniramine maleate

Learning Objectives

To understand the basic principle behind assay of compounds along with medicinal uses of compounds.

Principle

Potentiometric titration is a technique similar to direct **titration** of a **redox** reaction. It is a useful means of characterizing an acid. No **indicator** is used; instead the **potential** is measured across the **analyte**, typically an electrolyte solution. Chlorpheniramine, marketed in its salt **chlorpheniramine maleate**, is a first-generation alkyl amine antihistamine drug.

Use: Antihistaminic

Requirements

A) CHEMICALS

Perchloric acid, Anhydrous glacial acetic acid

B) APPARATUS

Beaker, Pipette, Burette, measuring cylinder, conical flask etc.

Procedure

Weigh accurately about 0.2 g and dissolve in 20 ml of anhydrous glacial acetic acid. Titrate with 0.1 M perchloric acid, determining the end-point potentiometrically. Carry out a blank titration.

1 ml of 0.1 M perchloric acid is equivalent to 0.01954 g of $C_{16}H_{19}ClN_2, C_4H_4O_4$.

Percentage purity= (Titre value x molarity of perchloric acid x Eq.factor) x 100

$$\overline{\text{Weight taken x expected molarity}}$$

Report

The % purity of Chlorpheniramine maleate was found to be......

Experiment No:21

ASSAY OF ISONICOTINIC ACID HYDRAZIDE

Aim: To determine percentage purity Isonicotinic acid hydrazide.

Learning Objectives

To understand the basic principle behind assay of compounds along with medicinal uses of compounds.

Principle

The reaction between INH in nonaqueous medium and acetic acid is an acid base reaction where the strong acid can donate a proton to nitrogen of the amino group of the drug molecule. In the presence of perchloric acid, acetic acid will accept a proton:

$$CH_3COOH + HClO_4 \rightleftharpoons CH_3COOH_2^+ + ClO_4^-,$$

$$CH_3COOH_2^+ + CH_3COO^- \rightleftharpoons 2CH_3COOH.$$

The $CH_3COOH_2^+$ can very readily give up its proton to react with a base, so basic properties of a base is enhanced and hence, titration between weak base and Since, INH is having basic nitrogen atoms in its molecular structure, the enhanced basicity of INH in acetic acid medium is due to non leveling effect of acetic acid, and the determination of INH becomes much easier. The procedure involves the titration of INH with perchloric acid with crystal violet as indicator.

$$(INH) \cdot 2H^+ + 2ClO_4^- \longrightarrow (INH) \cdot 2H^+ \cdot 2ClO_4^-$$

Possible reaction of neutralization.

Use: Antibiotic

Requirements

A) CHEMICALS

Acetic acid, INH, Perchloric acid, Crystal violet indicator.

B) APPARATUS

Beaker, Pipette, Burette, measuring cylinder, conical flask etc.

Procedure

Twenty tablets were weighed accurately and pulverized. A weighed quantity of the tablet powder equivalent to 150 mg INH was transferred into a clean and dry 100 mL volumetric flask. The flask was shaken for 20 min after adding 60 mL of acetic acid, the volume was brought to 100 mL with the same solvent. After 5 min, the solution was filtered through a Whatman No. 42 filter paper. First 10 mL of the aliquot was discarded.

10 mL aliquot of the drug solution containing 1.5–15.0 mg of INH was measured accurately and transferred into a clean and dry 100 mL titration flask. Two drops of crystal violet indicator were added and titrated with standard 0.02 M perchloric acid to a blue color end point. A blank titration was performed in the same manner without INH.

$$\text{Percentage purity} = \frac{(\text{Titre value} \times \text{molarity of perchloric acid} \times \text{Eq.factor}) \times 100}{\text{Weight taken} \times \text{expected molarity}}$$

Report

The % purity of Chlorpheniramine maleate was found to be......

References

1. N. Panda, A. K. Jena, J. Org. Chem., 2012, 77, 9401-9406.

2. Practical Heterocyclic Chemistry by A. O. Fitton and R. K. Smalley Academic Press London and New York, Page. 25.

3. Vogel's Textbook of Practical Organic Chemistry by Brian S. Furniss, Antony J. Hannaford, Peter W. G. Smith & Austin R. Tatchell; Fifth Edition; Page No.- 1162.

4. Vogel's Textbook of Practical Organic Chemistry by Brian S. Furniss, Antony J. Hannaford, Peter W. G. Smith & Austin R. Tatchell; Fifth Edition; Page No.- 1163.

5. Practical in organic chemistry, by Hitesh G. Raval, Sunil L. Baldania and Dimal A. Shah, Nirav Prakashan, Page No.- 303.

6. Vogel's Textbook of Practical Organic Chemistry by Brian S. Furniss, Antony J. Hannaford, Peter W. G. Smith & Austin R. Tatchell; Fifth Edition; Page No. 1190.

7. Vogel's Textbook of Practical Organic Chemistry by Brian S. Furniss, Antony J. Hannaford, Peter W. G. Smith & Austin R. Tatchell; Fifth Edition; Page No. 896

8. Vogel's Textbook of Practical Organic Chemistry by Brian S.

Furniss, Antony J. Hannaford, Peter W. G. Smith & Austin R. Tatchell
Fifth Edition; Page No. 1153.

9. Page.No.883, Vogel's Practical Organic Chemistry, 6th Edition.

10. Vogel's Textbook of Practical Organic Chemistry by Brian S
Furniss, Antony J. Hannaford, Peter W. G. Smith & Austin R. Tatchell
Fifth Edition; Page No. 1193.

11. Organic medical chemicals, by M. Barrowliff, 30-31, 1921.

12. Organic medical chemicals, by M. Barrowliff, 187, 1921.

Printed in Great Britain
by Amazon

67704991R00038